Sushi

A host of beautiful Japanese dishes

A QUANTUM BOOK

Published by
Chartwell Books
A Division of Book Sales, Inc.
114 Northfield Avenue
Edison, New Jersey, 08837
USA

ISBN 0-7858-0675-X

This book was produced by
Quantum Books Ltd
6 Blundell Street
London N7 9BH

Produced in Australia by Griffin Colour

Sushi

A host of beautiful Japanese dishes

KATSUJI YAMAMOTO
AND ROGER W HICKS

CHARTWELL
BOOKS, INC.

The Japanese have a genius for doing things beautifully. They also have a reputation for making things complicated. Who, for example, has not heard of the Japanese tea ceremony, which elevates a simple enough beverage into an art form?

Sushi can be almost as complicated as the tea ceremony, if you want to go into all the history and learn all the Japanese terms; and certainly, to become a master sushi chef (*itamae*) takes many years. On the other hand, you can learn enough about sushi to make it yourself at home surprisingly quickly. Many Japanese housewives do it all the time — although, of course, they apologize profusely for the fact that it is home-made.

INTRODUCTION

This is mainly a book about making your own sushi, but in order to appreciate sushi at home, you also need to know how to appreciate it when you eat out. There are all kinds of customs that are not immediately obvious: at the most basic, some people eat sushi 'set plates' for years before realizing that an *à la carte* order consists of two pieces, not one; or again, that if you are ordering *à la carte*, you do not order all the sushi you want at once. Instead, you order a few pieces, then a few more, and the meal is over when the *itamae* asks you if you want any more, and you say no. By watching the *itamae* you can also learn a great deal about making sushi at home!

It is also worth knowing a little about the history of sushi. One version says the rice was originally used to preserve fish, and was thrown away before the fish was eaten. Some people, however, acquired a taste for this rice, and that was the origin of sushi. Certainly, fermented fish dishes exist in many parts of Asia, including Japan: this is *nare-zushi* ('sushi' becomes 'zushi' when it is hyphenated like this).

Another version, first recorded 1,200 years ago, says the emperor Keiko was once served raw clams with vinegar and liked the taste so much he made the inventor his head chef.

Whatever the truth, there is no doubt sushi is enormously popular, and becoming more popular all the time. Even people who are squeamish about raw fish can become enthusiastic converts, once they realize that sushi rivals the finest fillet steak (*filet mignon*) in texture, and the flavor is exquisite. And, even if they do not want to try the more exotic varieties, such as octopus or sea-urchin, they can stick with tuna or yellowtail, vegetarian sushi of various kinds and even a 'kosher' roll made with smoked salmon and cream cheese.

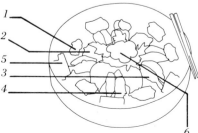

1 Ark shell
2 tuna
3 shrimp
4 mackerel
5 Egg Pancake
6 Spicy Tuna Roll.

NIGIRI-ZUSHI
AND
MAKI

The type of sushi that is best known in the West, and indeed which is most popular in Japan, is called *nigiri-zushi* or finger sushi. It first became popular about 200 years ago as a fast food – but what an improvement over Western fast food!

Nigiri-zushi is what most people mean when they say 'sushi,' and in many ways it is the simplest form, at least in concept. The chef carves a piece of raw fish (or any one of a number of other ingredients), puts a smear of *wasabi* (Japanese horseradish or Japanese mustard) on the bottom and places it on a little finger-shaped patty of vinegared sushi rice. Sometimes, there will be a 'strap' of *nori* (seaweed paper) around it as well. The whole thing is just solid enough to stay together in the fingers or when picked up with chopsticks, but it seems to melt when it is placed in your mouth. Needless to say, this is not quite as easy to prepare as it looks, but it is still something you can learn to do quite satisfactorily at home.

If the topping is soft or semi-liquid, as with some kinds of roe or sea urchin, the sushi-chef will build a little 'wall' of *nori* all the way around; such sushi are known as *gunkan-maki* or 'battleship sushi' from their resemblance to a man-of-war or battleship.

The next most usual kind of sushi is probably rolled sushi (*maki-zushi*). There are countless varieties of these, and sushi-chefs often have specialties which they have developed themselves. At the simplest, though, they consist of a sheet of *nori*, spread with sushi rice. In the center, the chef puts fish, avocado, cucumber or anything else suitable, then rolls the whole thing up in a tight roll with the help of a flexible bamboo mat. The roll is then sliced which in the more expensive restaurants are arranged very artistically.

The most spectacular kinds of rolled sushi may have an additional layer of rice outside the *nori*, with fish and sometimes avocado rolled on the outside of this. This is where chefs like to show their vituosity!

A more casual variety of *maki-zushi* is the hand-rolled *maki*, which usually looks like an old-fashioned ice-cream cone rolled from *nori* and filled with sushi rice, and whatever takes the fancy of the customer or the sushi-chef. Strictly, any *maki* which is not pressed with the bamboo mat is *temaki*.

With any form of rolled sushi, a single roll, which may be cut into anything up to eight pieces constitutes an order *à la carte*.

Finally, there are various other kinds of finger sushi such as *inari* (stuffed fried tofu), Tiger Eye and cooked sushi.

Hako-zushi (box sushi) is made using a special pressing box with a removable top and base.

OTHER TYPES OF SUSHI AND SASHIMI

Scattered Sushi *(Chirashi-zushi)*

As you might expect, the way in which the ingredients are 'scattered' in *chirashi-zushi* is rarely careless. This is, however, the very simplest type of sushi to make, if you are not too worried about the aesthetics.

Almost anything can be used in *chirashi-zushi*. As well as fish, you can use vegetables, omelet, chicken, scrambled egg and *shiitake* mushrooms.

Steamed Sushi *(Mushi-zushi)*

If you make *chirashi-zushi* with raw, soaked rice, and then steam it in a bowl for 15 minutes, you have *mushi-zushi*. This is one of the few types of sushi which can be re-heated as 'leftovers' – though it still won't keep for more than a day or two in the refrigerator.

Box Sushi *(Hako-zushi)*

Hako-zushi requires a pressing-box, as illustrated. It may be made with one or more kinds of fish, but differs from *nigiri-zushi* in that the rice and fish are pressed into one big block, which is then sliced up for serving.

Fermented Sushi *(Nare-zushi)*

Nare-zushi has already been mentioned as one of the possible origins of sushi. Although it is still made in some districts of Japan, it is something of an acquired taste, and is not conveniently, or safely, made at home. Some types of fermented sushi take a year to reach the right stage of aging.

Sashimi

Sashimi is effectively sushi without the rice. The fish may be raw or cooked, marinated or unmarinated. Some types can take a little getting used to: whole baby squid taste delicious, but they look somewhat unnerving to a Western eye.

Sashimi is sometimes eaten as a prelude to sushi, sometimes as an appetizer to a cooked meal and sometimes in its own right.

SUSHI TECHNIQUES

In this book, we have consciously restricted ourselves to presenting sushi which could be made at home. Up to a certain point, sushi is a matter of technique. Beyond that point, it is pure art. What you are paying for in the very best sushi restaurants in Tokyo is not the ingredients, or even the *ambiance* of the restaurant; it is the grace and skill with which the ingredients are arranged.

While this sort of a presentation adds greatly to the experience of eating in a great sushi restaurant, it is easy to be intimidated by such artistry. Instead, build on the basic techniques taught here. Watch the *itamae* at work when you eat out, and, in time, you can start to worry about art as well as technique.

Above all else, the secret of sushi-making is to keep your hands wet. Otherwise, the fish will dry out and the rice will stick to your fingers. This was a recurrent problem throughout the photography for this book: an *itamae* normally works fast, and slowing down means dried-out sushi. Add about 2 tbsp vinegar to 2 cups water in a bowl, and float a slice of lemon in it. Wet your hands and your knife with this.

Knives are used wet, and cleaned frequently. Either wipe the blade with a damp cloth, or dip the tip in water and tap the handle on the counter, holding the knife upright, to spread the water. Take great care not to transfer flavors, especially onion, to other ingredients with the knife.

Trim all fish mercilessly, both for aesthetics and for the palate; shreds of skin, bones and discolored parts have no place in sushi. With fatty fish, trim off the very dark meat by the belly, as this is too strongly flavored for most people.

Sushi chefs use a pair of heavy flat-ended tweezers to remove bones from filleted fish. Check visually and with the tips of your fingers.

When cutting fish from a squared-off fillet (the form in which it is often bought), slice the end piece as shown opposite, do not use it for *nigiri-zushi* because it will not be as tender as a piece cut on the bias, and it will not look right. This technique is known as *sakudori*. Awkward-shaped scraps can be used in rolls, where appearance is not important.

Long chopsticks for cooking are not essential, but they can be very useful. Wooden ones are used for beating the eggs for omelets and for manipulating the omelet in the pan, while the sort with fine metal tips are useful for making the final adjustments to finished sushi.

Small pieces of sushi look less impressive than large pieces, are more work, and dry out faster; but they are easier to eat in a single mouthful.

Fish is always cut on the bias, like this.

The easiest way to divide a sheet of nori *is with a knife – don't attempt to break it by hand.*

Vegetables are often diced from short lengths; this is much easier than trying to dice a long, tapering vegetable.

Keep a bowl of water with a slice of lemon to hand for wetting the knife.

FILLETING FISH

There are two ways to fillet a fish for sushi. The first, used for most fish except flatfish, *sanmai oroshi* gives three fillets and a skeleton. The second *gomai oroshi* is used for flatfish and for larger fish, and is described in detail overleaf.

Three-piece Fillet
(Sanmai Oroshi)

If the fish requires scaling (this one does not, it is served with the skin on), hold the head of the fish firmly and scrape off the scales – be careful as you will be cutting towards yourself. Clean both sides. Alternatively, hold the tail. Do not hold the body, as this will bruise the flesh and destroy its firmness. Throughout the process, wash frequently in lightly salted water.

1 Place the fish with the head facing to the left (if right-handed). With a sharp knife, make a diagonal cut at the base of the head to remove it.

2 Slice backwards along the belly towards the anal (pelvic) fin.

3 Remove the stomach and viscera.

5 Taking the piece of fish containing the backbone, rest the left hand gently on the fish and slide the knife along the back between the flesh and bone from the head to the tail.

4 Rest the left hand lightly on top of the fish and cut along the back from head to the tail so that the knife skims the rib cage. Lift off the fillet.

6 Reverse the fish and cut through the base of the tail, releasing the second fillet. Pluck out any bones remaining in the fillets.

7 The fish is now in three pieces: a left and a right fillet, and a skeleton. If the fillets are very large, cut them in half lengthwise – or, of course, use the *gomai oroshi* described overleaf.

FILLETING FISH

Five-piece Fillet *(Gomai Oroshi)*

There are two variations of five-piece filleting technique. One is used for flatfish, and the other for large fish such as bonita, a member of the tuna family. If you try to bone large fish *sanmai oroshi*, you run the risk of damaging the flesh by trying to remove too large a fillet at once. Bruised fish with 'shakes' in the flesh is no good for sushi.

VARIATION 1: FLATFISH

1 Resting the left hand (if you are right handed) on the head of the fish, make two deep cuts behind the gills.

2 Turn the fish and remove the head. Squeeze out the stomach and viscera and clean the fish thoroughly under cold running water.

3 Turn the fish again, and cut down to the spine from head to tail.

4 Keeping the knife blade flat, slide it along the bone to release the flesh.

With a large fish like tuna or, as here, bonita, you first gut the fish and remove the head, then proceed as in the following steps:

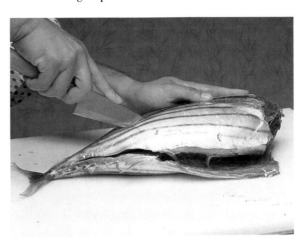

5 Starting from the tail, slide the knife along the outside edge of the fish to release the first fillet. Reverse the fish and follow steps 3 to 5 to remove the second fillet from the top of the fish.

1 Make a long cut along the lateral line from head to tail.

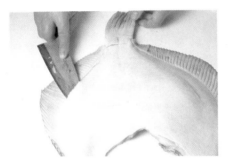

6 Turn the fish over and again remove a left and a right fillet.

2 Make a second incision, coming down from the spine. Remove the fillet.

7 The result is a fish in five pieces, as shown. You will also have four pieces of *engawa*, the meat next to the side fins. *Engawa* is much prized, but only a large fish will provide enough to be worth using.

3 Remove the belly fillet by cutting from above. Repeat steps 1 to 3 for the other side.

VEGETABLES

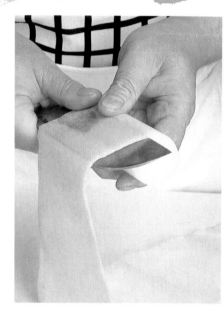

Daikon *and other vegetables are sometimes peeled in a long continuous sheet. The sheet is then cut into 8in lengths, stacked and finely sliced to make an edible 'angel hair' garnish.*

Pickled daikon (radish), cucumber, avocado, wakegi (scallion) and root ginger.

Avocado: Using avocados in sushi is a comparatively recent innovation. Predictably, they are especially popular in California, one of the world's leading producers. Avocado is delicious in *maki* (rolls) of various kinds, and is also used to add color to a Rainbow Roll.

Carrots (ninjin): As with avocados, carrots are used both for their culinary value and for their color. They are a prime ingredient in Vegetable Rolls.

Cucumber (kappa): Cucumbers are a classic ingredient in Vegetable Rolls, and are also widely used as a garnish. Japanese cucumbers are smaller and less watery than the larger British and American varieties.

Daikon: Sometimes called a 'radish,' this is much bigger and milder than the small red radish familiar to most westerners. If you cannot find it anywhere else, try Indian and Pakistani shops: the name in Hindi is *mooli*.

Kampyō: Dried gourd.

Natto: A kind of glutinous soya bean preparation, not readily available (or widely liked) in the West.

Onion (wakegi): Green onions or scallions are sometimes used in the more modern forms of sushi. A Kosher Roll, for example, contains smoked salmon, cream cheese and green onions. Generally, though, onion overwhelms the delicate taste of sushi.

Seaweed: In sushi, the most usual seaweed is the dark green or black *nori*. It is effectively a kind of paper made from chopped, dried purple laver, and is used to wrap sushi. It rapidly loses its aroma unless it is frozen, in which case it is good for two or three months or more. Before use, lightly toast one side of the sheet of *nori* to bring out the flavor; about 30 seconds over a gas flame is ideal. Toasting both sides seems to diminish the taste again. A full sheet of *nori* is 7×8¼in.

Ao nori is a flaked version of the same thing, used as a seasoning.

Kombu is used to make *dashi* soup stock.

Shütake mushrooms are sometimes used in sushi.

Fresh wasabi *(Japanese horseradish or Japanese mustard) like this, left, is very hard to obtain outside Japan. Prepared* wasabi *or powdered* wasabi *are the alternatives.*

OTHER INGREDIENTS

Dark soy sauce is used for general cooking purposes, while the lighter variety (on the right) is used where coloring is not required.

Japanese su *(rice vinegar) should always be used when available, but diluted cider vinegar may be substituted.*

Mirin *(sweetened cooking sake) can be bought ready-made in bottles.*

Bean curd (tōfu): Basic tofu no longer needs special introduction: the creamy-white cubes are a familiar sight in many Western supermarkets and health food shops. The kind of tofu used in *Inari* is, however deep fried.

Some people use tofu instead of rice under *nigiri-zushi*; it is very good for you, but rather bland. Well-flavored fish and spicy condiments are advisable.

Cream cheese: A very un-Japanese ingredient (the Japanese share the usual Oriental view of 'rotten milk') which is nevertheless making more and more appearances in various kinds of *maki*.

Eggs: Chicken eggs are used to make *Tamago* omelets and quail eggs are used as a garnish, for example with roe. A *Sake* Shooter is a quail egg yolk in the bottom of a glass of *sake*.

Katsuo-bushi: Dried bonito flakes used to make *dashi* soup stock.

Mirin: Also known as 'sweet *sake*,' this is used for a number of purposes, including cooking sushi rice. If you cannot get *mirin*, dissolve heaped ½ cup sugar in ½-1 cup hot dry *sake*.

Miso: Fermented soya bean paste. The lighter varieties tend to be less salty and sweeter than the darker varieties.

Pickled plums (ume-boshi): Sometimes used in vegetarian *maki*.

Rice vinegar (su): Japanese rice vinegar is pale straw in color and very mild; do not confuse it with red or black rice vinegar, which are strongly flavored. Wine, cider and malt vinegars are too strong for most Japanese dishes – diluted cider vinegar can be used, though.

Soy sauce (shōyu): Japanese or American soy sauces are more delicate than Chinese. Regular dark soy sauce (*koi kuchi shōyu*) is normally used; if you are on a low-sodium diet, use the sodium-reduced variety, but do not confuse it with *usui kuchi shōyu* which is lighter in color but higher in salt content than *koi kuchi shōyu*.

Sugar: Even those who love Japanese food are sometimes shocked to discover how much sugar it contains. In sushi, sugar is used in rice preparation and in making some kinds of glaze.

Sake *is the national alcoholic drink of Japan and is the most suitable accompaniment to a Japanese meal, after authentic Japanese tea.*

DASHI AND SOUP

Dashi is one of the fundamental ingredients of much Japanese cooking. It is encountered less with sushi than with other dishes, but it is still used in preparing several kinds of cooked ingredients and for soup.

Dashi

The ingredients are simple: *katsuo-bushi* (dried bonito flakes), *kombu* (seaweed) and water. Traditionally, *katsuo-bushi* comes in a block like a mahogany plank and is shaved for use. Today, however, most people buy ready-made flakes. Check the expiry date because anything over six months old will be past its prime.

■ The proportions are also simple in dry measure, ½ cup *katsuo-bushi* per 1 cup water, seasoned with 2–3sq in.

■ Put the *kombu* in a pot with the cold water, then bring to a boil. As soon as the water begins to boil, remove the *kombu*. Leaving the *kombu* in makes the stock bitter and cloudy.

■ Add the *katsuo-bushi* to the stock and turn up the heat. Do not stir. As soon as the stock is boiling again, remove the pan from the heat. When the *katsuo-bushi* flakes sink, the dashi is ready. Strain the flakes out; leaving them in will make the *dashi* too fishy. Both the *kombu* and the *katsuo-bushi* can be re-used to make a less strongly flavored *dashi*.

■ Vary the quantities of *katsuo-bushi* to suit your individual taste; at first, many Westerners use less. You may also care to mix *dashi* with chicken, beef or even vegetable stock.

Soups

Although there are many kinds of soup with a *dashi* base, the ones usually encountered with sushi are *suimono* and *miso-dashi*.

SUIMONO

To make *suimono*, heat *dashi* with a little *tofu* (bean curd), fish or chicken. If you are using *tofu*, do not allow the soup to boil or the *tōfu* will disintegrate. Add either a few flakes of seaweed or a chopped scallion. In a classic *suimono*, there is also a seasonal garnish (*sui-kichi*) such as pepper leaves, but this is both perfectionist and unnecessarily difficult in the West.

MISO-DASHI

Miso-dashi is much the same thing, thickened with about 2tbsp *miso* to 2 cups *dashi*. *Miso-dashi* may be made with *tōfu*, seasonal vegetables or seafood.

Kombu *comes as leathery, dried strips of seaweed. Although* katsuo boshi *is traditionally sold in a solid block which is shaved for use, most people now buy it ready-shaved.*

A beautifully garnished miso-dashi *made with* tōfu *and leeks.*

KAMPYŌ AND SHIITAKE

Kampyō is made from the dried skin of a Japanese gourd and is packaged in long strips. It is used in some kinds of *maki* (rolls) and in *chirashi-zushi* (scattered sushi), as well as in other recipes.

To reconstitute *kampyō*, wash a small amount in water with a scrubbing motion and rub with salt. Soak for at least a couple of hours, or overnight. To cook and season *kampyō* for use in sushi, boil it – about 10 minutes, until it is translucent, then simmer for about 5 minutes in *dashi* (page 36) seasoned with 1tbsp sugar, 1½tsp soy sauce, and a pinch of salt for each 1 cup *dashi*.

Shiitake mushrooms are normally sold dried. They smell quite strong and are very expensive but are essential for an authentic Japanese flavor in some dishes. In any case, most of the smell vanishes when they are soaked. They also gain considerably in weight after soaking; a small amount of dried *shiitake* will last a long time and go a long way.

If you are in a hurry, you can soak *shiitake* mushrooms for as little as 30–40 minutes, then remove the hard cores and stems before cooking. Soaking overnight – 24 hours is fine – allows you to use the whole mushroom and makes for greater tenderness.

To prepare seasoned *shiitake* mushrooms for serving use the following recipe:

INGREDIENTS

4–6 shiitake mushrooms, well soaked and squeezed dry with ⅔ cup soaking liquid reserved

1 cup *dashi*

dash of sake – about 1tsp

2tbsp sugar

1tbsp soy sauce

1tbsp *mirin*

METHOD

■ Mix the mushroom liquid, the *dashi* and the *sake*. Bring to a boil in a heavy-based pan, then add the mushrooms. Reduce heat to a simmer and cook about 3 minutes, basting frequently.

■ Add the sugar and continue to simmer until the liquid has been reduced to half (this should take less than 10 minutes). Add the soy sauce and cook for another 3–4 minutes, then add the *mirin*. Continue cooking over a high heat, shaking the pan, until the mushrooms are evenly coated with glaze.

Kampyō, *before and after preparation*

Shiitake *mushrooms*

GARNISHES

The line between ingredients and garnishes can be hard to draw: after all, a sushi meal is an aesthetic whole.

Kappa (cucumber): Cutting vegetables for garnishes is an essential part of Japanese cuisine, and one of the most exquisite techniques involves the 'pine-tree' cut shown here.

1 Using the end of a cucumber, score parallel lines of equal length lengthwise.

2 Cut at right angles, with the knife parallel to the board.

3 Push the cut part to one side.

4 Repeat, pushing the cut parts alternately left and right.

5 Decorate with smelt roe for real color.

Strips of gari (above) can be rolled up to create a 'rose' for garnishing (right).

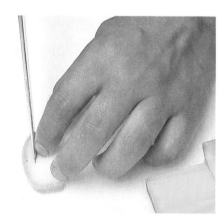

1 Take a slice of kamaboko and cut a slit along the center of the slice. To form a 'plait,' insert one end of the slice through the slit and pull under.

2 To make a 'knot,' take a slice of kamaboko and cut a slit as above. Cut 2 oblong 'sticks' from another slice of kamboko and tuck into the slit to create 'ends.'

3 A block of kamaboko, with a 'plait' and two 'knot' garnishes.

Daikon: Cutting *daikon* into ornamental shapes is also a common practice; many of the techniques for *daikon* are also applicable to carrot, and some can also be used on cucumber.

The easiest way to produce the flower-shape is to use a small device like a cookie cutter, though a traditional-minded chef will carve cylinders 2in long and then slice them. Another technique involves shaving off a 'thick peel' as though you were using a pencil sharpener; the 'thick peel' can then be cut on the bias and will curl attractively.

Gari (pickled ginger): Known to sushi-lovers as *gari* rather than the conventional Japanese *shōga*, this pink pickled root ginger is eaten in small quantities between orders to clear the palate and increase the appreciation of the next order.

Goma (sesame seeds): These are used at the discretion of the *itamae* to enhance certain kinds of sushi. For the best flavor, they should be dry roasted or toasted in a hot cast-iron pan for about a minute before they are used; keep them moving to avoid popping and burning. *Shiro goma* and *muki goma* are respectively unhulled and hulled white sesame seeds.

Oba: The beefsteak plant gives this hearty-looking leaf, prized both for its appearance and its scent.

Hiyashi-wakame: A type of seaweed. It is sold dried but is soaked and shredded to give a slippery, bright-green garnish.

Kamaboko (fish cake): *Kamaboko* is frequently used as an edible garnish. You can make 'knots' or 'braids' by cutting a slit in the middle of a strip of fish cake, and then either forcing the end of the strip through the slot to create a plait or making two more cuts (to create 'ends') and pushing them through the slit.

Wasabi: Sometimes called 'Japanese horseradish' because it is derived from a root, the name 'Japanese mustard' describes the taste better. Fresh root is extremely difficult to find, and very expensive, but dried powdered *wasabi* is readily available and affordable.

S U S H I   R I C E

Sushi rice is made from a matured short-grain rice. Some sushi chefs even have their rice merchants mix rice of differing degrees of maturity to achieve the desired result.

Rice is best cooked in about its own weight of water: very new rice, which contains more moisture, requires less, and older rice may require more. Experiment to get the best results. You will find it easier if you stick with a single brand of rice, as the moisture content is likely to be more constant.

■ Wash the rice thoroughly until the water comes clear. Let the washed rice dry and swell for an hour.

■ To cook rice easily, you need a pot with a tight-fitting lid. Bring the rice to a boil over medium heat, then cover tightly. Boil over a high flame for 2 minutes, then a medium flame for 5 minutes, and a low flame for about 15 minutes to absorb the remaining water. You should be able to hear the different stages of cooking: at first, the rice bubbles, but when all the water has been absorbed, it begins to hiss. Never remove the lid during cooking if you want the very best rice.

■ Once the rice has cooked, remove the lid, drape a teacloth over the top of the pan and let it cool for 10–15 minutes.

The cooked and cooled rice is poured into a *hangiri*.

■ Pour the rice into a *hangiri* (cedarwood rice-cooling tub) or other non-metallic container. Spread it out evenly with a *shamoji* (rice-paddle) or large wooden spoon.

■ Run the *shamoji* through the rice as though you were ploughing a field, first left-to-right and then top-to-bottom, again and again. This is to separate the grains. As you do so, add the *sushi-zu*; ⅔cup will treat 1½–2lb *uncooked* rice. Do not add too much: the rice should just stick together without being mushy.

■ At the same time, you need to fan the rice to cool it and help it separate – the action will also add a gloss to the grains. Unless you have three hands, you will need an assistant with an *uchiwa* (a fan) or an un-romantic but equally effective piece of cardboard. It takes about 10 minutes to get the rice thoroughly mixed and down to room temperature.

2 Using a *shamoji*, or large wooden spoon, quickly and lightly toss and cut the rice to separate the individual grains.

3 At the same time add the *sushi-zu*.

If you cannot get ready-made *sushi-zu* (sushi vinegar), dissolve 5tbsp sugar in a little more than 5tbsp rice vinegar with 2–4tsp salt (the higher quantity is more traditional). You will have to first heat the vinegar to get the sugar to dissolve, then cool rapidly by plunging the bowl into cold water, to avoid distilling off the vinegar.

NIGIRI-ZUSHI TECHNIQUE

'*Nigiri*' literally means 'squeezing,' and that is what you do. Left-handers should follow a mirror image of the sequence given below; Japan is a strongly right-handed society.

There are several classic shapes for making the 'pillow' of rice, including *kushi-gata* or *rikyu-gata* (elongated dome), *ogi-gata* (fan shape, a flattened version of *kushi-gata*), *funa-gata* (boat-shaped, with a flat top, a curved bottom, and punt-like squared-off bow and transom, as shown here), *tawara-gata* (lightly compressed to give a fat sausage shape like a rice bale or long cotton bale), and *hako-gata* (box-shaped). The first two are the most usual, and the last two are rare.

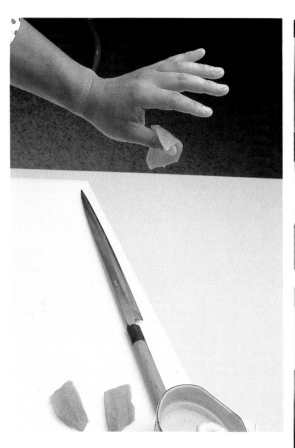

1 Pick up the topping with the left hand. Pick up a ball of rice with your right hand; the rice-tub should be on your right side. Round the ball of rice against the wall of the rice-tub. At this stage, uncompressed, the ball should be around the size of a golf ball or ping-pong ball.

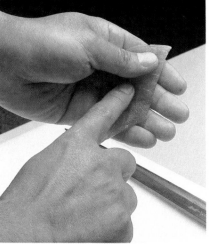

2 With the rice ball in the palm of your right hand, pick up a dab of *wasabi* on your right index finger and smear it on the center of the underside of the topping.

3 Put the rice ball onto the topping. Keeping the fingers of the left hand flat, lightly press the rice under the topping. Your thumb will leave a small depression in the ball.

4 Squeeze the sides with your right hand.

5 Curling your left hand around the sushi, with the left thumb as shown, press down with the first two fingers of your right hand to squeeze it flat.

6 Transfer the sushi to your other hand.

7 Replace it in the left hand, but end-over-end: the part that was squeezed by your thumb is now at the open side of the hand.

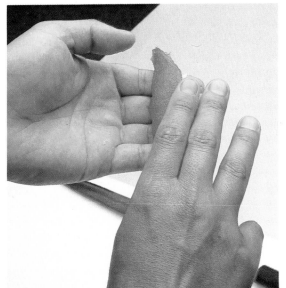

8 Repeat step 5 above: this evens up the other end of the sushi.

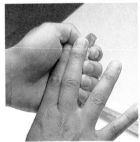

9 Roll the sushi from the cup of your hand to the fingers, so the topping is on top.

10 Give a final squeeze to even out the shape.

MAKI

TECHNIQUE

Gunkan-maki ('battleship sushi') has already been mentioned.

Temaki is made on a strip of *nori* (seaweed paper) 1in wide; a little sushi rice and some topping are laid on top, and the roll is wrapped and stuck as for *gunkan-maki*.

Other forms of *maki* are made with a *makisu* (bamboo rolling mat). The tight-rolled *maki* include small *maki* or *hoso-maki*, as illustrated here.

The basic technique for *hoso-maki* is this:

When cutting a roll, if you have any particularly ingredients which might make neat cutting difficult, such as carrot or *kampyō*, cut down with a steady slicing motion until you encounter resistance, then hit the back of the blade smartly with your free hand to complete the cut.

1 Put a half sheet *nori* on the *makisu*, then cover with a layer of sushi rice about ⅜in thick. Go all the way to the sides but leave the top and bottom of the *nori* uncovered.

2 Put the topping onto the rice; several toppings are often mixed. This is burdock root, which is hot and crunchy (it is available canned in some Oriental stores). *Goma* (sesame seeds) are added here for flavor. If you were making a fish roll, you would add *wasabi* (Japanese horseradish).

3 Roll the *maki* up in the *makisu*, starting from the edge nearest you.

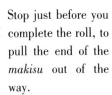

4 Stop just before you complete the roll, to pull the end of the *makisu* out of the way.

5 Finish rolling with the *makisu*. Compress the roll: some people square the roll, while others leave it round.

6 Push in the ends if they are untidy.

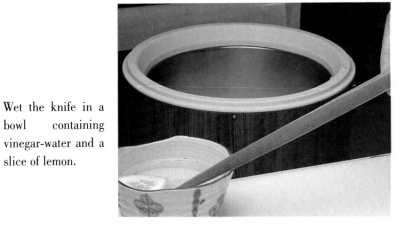 

7 Wet the knife in a bowl containing vinegar-water and a slice of lemon.

8 Tap the butt of the knife on the table to spread the vinegar-water over the blade's surface.

9 Cut the roll in half and lay the two halves side by side.

10 Divide each half into 3 equal sections, giving 6 slices in all.

1 The *awabi* does not look promising.

2 Cut out the mouth parts.

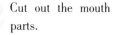

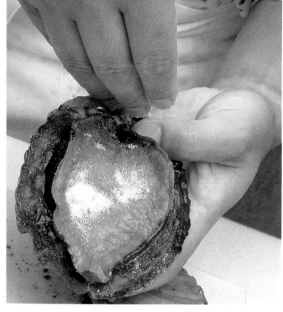

3 Sprinkle generously with salt. Tap the shell to make sure the salt penetrates everywhere. After a minute or so, the flesh will be contracted and rigid.

4 Carefully cut the *awabi* out of the shell with a sharp knife.

5 Remove the entrails. The stomach, sliced raw and mixed with *ponzu* (citrus vinegar) and a little scallion is regarded as a delicacy. Some people even eat the rest of the entrails, though these are normally cooked.

6 Scrub the main body of the *awabi* with a brush and plenty of salt. It is now perfectly clean.

7 Remove the dark fringe around the edge of the flesh. On a large abalone, this will be too tough to be edible.

8 If the *awabi* is big enough, remove the small muscle on top for the very best sushi. Otherwise, slice the whole fish diagonally.

ABALONE
(*AWABI*)

Awabi (abalone) is regarded as one of the great delicacies of sushi. Before about 1950, it was normally cooked before serving, but today the most highly prized form is the fresh, raw *awabi*.

The smaller the awabi, the more tender the flesh. *Awabi* of 4in or under can be sliced whole: bigger ones are prepared as shown.

Abalone are widely distributed in temperate and tropical seas, especially around Australia. They are also found along the West Coast of North America and off Japan, the Channel Islands, the west coast of France, and in the Mediterranean, as well as China and the Canary Islands. They are reckoned to be at their best in April, May and June. They live on the seabed near the *kombu* and *nori* on which they feed – an apparent example of predestination . . . The Sea Cradle, Gum Boot or Giant Chiton (related to the limpet) can be prepared as for *awabi*.

1 Spread a thin layer (about ⅜in) of sushi rice on a half sheet of *nori* (seaweed paper). Sprinkle with *goma* (sesame seeds).

2 Turn the whole thing over and smear a little *wasabi* (Japanese horseradish) on the *nori*.

3 Strips of finely sliced cucumber and avocado are added first in the middle.

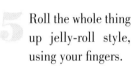

4 Crab meat completes the contents.

5 Roll the whole thing up jelly-roll style, using your fingers.

8 A garnish of smelt roe is not essential, but it does make the roll more colorful.

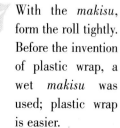

6 Place a piece of plastic wrap over it.

7 With the *makisu*, form the roll tightly. Before the invention of plastic wrap, a wet *makisu* was used; plastic wrap is easier.

CALIFORNIA ROLL
AND
VEGETABLE ROLL

As its name suggests, California Roll is hardly a classical sushi recipe. It is, however, extremely popular on the West Coast of the United States, and has made progress not only on the East Coast but even in Tokyo. It is a superb blend of textures: cooked crab, avocado and cucumber. Also, of course, it appeals to people who want to try sushi but are not sure about raw fish.

Although it is quite possible to make a *hoso-maki* roll in this way, there is not much space available for filling if you do. Consequently, it is usual to make these rolls inside-out.

Inside-out Vegetable Rolls are more traditional than California Rolls, but generally less popular in the West. Instead of the cucumber-avocado-crab filling, the traditional ingredients are cucumber or seasoned *kampyō*.
You may wish to try other ingredients, including finely sliced carrot, snow peas and even cream cheese.

For presentation, the California Roll is carefully sliced into six pieces. The end pieces, with the ends protruding, are normally placed in the middle.

HALIBUT (Hirame) AND SALMON (Sake)

Various types of flatfish are served as sushi, but they are all served the same way. Depending on where you live, the same or very similar fishes may be called halibut, plaice or flounder – though the halibut is normally much bigger. Flatfish sometimes appear on sushi bar menus under the unappetizing name of 'fluke'.

The Japanese flatfish is small, more like a plaice or flounder, but the big *hirame* (halibut) is prepared in the same way.

Most species are reckoned to be at their best in winter, with autumn as the second season of choice.

The flesh may simply be sliced and served as *nigiri-zushi* with no further preparation, or it may be briefly marinated in a sauce made of scallion, *momigi oroshi* (hot-pepper paste in vinegar) and *ponzu* (citrus vinegar).

Ponzu is obtainable ready-to-use from Japanese shops, or you can make a substitute by adding 1 cup orange juice and the juice of 1 lemon to 4½ cups *zu* (rice vinegar).

At the Yamato, *ponzu* is not used alone. To make a useful sauce, which can be used with fish or as a basis for powerful soup (*suimono*), bring 4½ cups *ponzu* to the boil with *kombu* and *katsuo-bushi*, add an equal volume of soy sauce and ½ cup *mirin*, then strain.

Where salmon is served as sashimi, the presentation is much the same as for flatfish. In Japan, salmon is hardly ever served raw, and California is probably the only area where it is really popular. Cod and rock cod can be served the same way. Shark could also be prepared by the same techniques, but most people find it too fishy tasting.

Hirame *and salmon served as* nigiri-zushi.

DEEP-FRIED TOFU (*Inari*)

Inari are somewhat bland pockets of tofu which have been deep-fried, then braised. They are stuffed with sushi rice, with or without the addition of *goma* (sesame seeds) or *gari* (pickled ginger). They are something of an acquired taste, but they are economical and they keep well, making them popular as a light packed lunch.

Age (tofu pouches) are bought already deep-fried; they are available frozen or refrigerated in some Oriental markets. They are very perishable and should be used within a couple of days if they are not kept frozen. They are first blanched in boiling water for a few seconds to remove excess oil, then drained and dried on paper towels. While they are still warm, cut in half.

To create the pocket, put a half-pouch in the palm of one hand, and slap it smartly with the other hand; loosening the middle. You can now open it up gently to create a deep pouch.

INGREDIENTS OF
BRAISING STOCK FOR *AGE*

This is enough stock (broth) for 8 half pouches

½ cup *dashi*
heaped ½ cup sugar
3tbsp soy sauce
2tbsp *sake*

METHOD

■ Mix all the ingredients together in a large saucepan, heating until the sugar is dissolved. Braise the pouches in this for 6–7 minutes, basting frequently to avoid scorching. Cool to room temperature, without draining. When cool, drain.

The name *inari* comes from folk-lore. The fox which supposedly guarded the temples of the god Inari was said to be especially fond of *age*, so sushi made from *age* are named after the god. Sometimes, they are called 'Fox Sushi', from the same legend.

Open the braised pouch.

2 Fill with sushi rice and compress the rice with the thumb.

Present the *inari* with the flap tucked under.

RAINBOW ROLL

The Rainbow Roll is the most colorful of the inside-out rolls which have become popular since the 1950s. The only easy way to make them is with the aid of plastic wrap. Before the advent of plastic wrap, they were sometimes made using a cloth or a second wetted *makisu* (bamboo rolling mat), but the whole process is much easier with plastic wrap.

The technique and inside ingredients are the same as for the California Roll. In fact, at the Yamato, the Rainbow Roll is on the menu as a California Special Roll.

Once you have your basic inside-out roll, place strips of different-colored fish and avocado on top of the roll; they must be very thinly sliced, but thick enough to show the color. Garnish with sesame seeds if you like; black ones are dramatic.

Put more plastic wrap around the whole thing, and roll once again in the *makisu*. Remove the plastic wrap and slice – or, if you are feeling cowardly, remove the plastic wrap *after* slicing.

1 Choose the fish for color: white fish like halibut, creamy-colored fish like yellowtail, fresh orange or smoked salmon, red bonita. Slice very thinly.

2 Alternate the colors for maximum effect.

3 Squeeze in a *makisu* after wrapping it with plastic wrap.

SCATTERED SUSHI
(Chirashi-zushi)

The *chirashi-zushi* (scattered sushi) illustrated here is the *Kanto-fu Chirashi-zushi*; Kanto is the eastern part of Japan, and it is where *chirashi-zushi* originated. It consists of nothing more than a bed of plain sushi rice, on which are placed various kinds of fish, together with thick *tomago* (omelet), *kampyō* (dried gourd) and *shiitake* mushrooms.

Another form of *chirashi-zushi* is made by mixing all the ingredients together with *gomoku-zushi*, though in western Japan (Kansai) it is known simply as *chirashi-*

zushi again. Another name for *gomoku-zushi* is therefore *Kansai-fu Chirashi-zushi*.

Because there are so many ways of making it, preparation of *chirashi-zushi* is more a question of state of mind than of following a recipe. Just keep experimenting until you find the mixture that suits you best. One of the simplest forms of *gomoku-zushi*, for example, is *kani* (crab) *chirashi-zushi*, a rice salad mixed with the crab. For ½lb crab meat (sprinkled with the juice of half a small lemon), use the following quantities:

INGREDIENTS

2½ cups cooked sushi rice

2 cucumbers

2 large *shiitake* mushrooms

2oz *renkon* (lotus root), peeled, available from Oriental shops tinned

3 tamago, thinly sliced

reduced *dashi*

½tsp salt

1tsp sugar

PREPARATION

■ Slice the cucumbers thinly and reduce their moisture by 'sweating' them under a fine sprinkling of salt for a few minutes, then washing in fresh water and squeezing dry. Soak the lotus root in vinegared water for 10 minutes.

■ Boil just enough water to cover all the slices and add a pinch of salt and a dash of water. Blanch the slices for about 30 seconds, then drain and marinate in reduced *dashi* or water with the salt and sugar.

■ Mix all the ingredients together, reserving a few for garnish. Or, use *kamaboko* (fish cake) or more crab as a garnish. Or, garnish with boiled shrimp, sliced eel, gizzard, shad, tuna and squid, *tamago* (omelet), more *shiitake* and lotus root, prepared as above and 1 cucumber, prepared as above. *Gari* and *wasabi* can be added to taste, and of course you can always add *kampyō* to any *chirashi-zushi*.

■ Other forms of *chirashi-zushi* are made with deep-fried tofu, green beans, bamboo shoots and even chicken.

SEA EEL
(Anago)
AND
EEL
(Unagi)

Unagi (eel) is cooked before being used to make sushi. The *anago* is the famous conger eel, but you want only small specimens. The giant mankillers do not taste so good, and are in any case inconvenient to handle and cook. A good *unagi* is even smaller, and weighs only 5–6oz.

Filleting *unagi* is different from filleting other fish. The easiest way to do it is to pin the head down on a chopping board, with the backbone towards you. Make an incision with a sharp knife just above the backbone, behind the head, and cut from head to tail. Lift this fillet carefully and flip it over onto the chopping board.

Cut through the backbone just behind the head, and holding the knife parallel to the chopping board, slide it under the backbone from head to tail. Remove the backbone and entrails and scrape the slimy skin with the back of the knife. Rinse and drain.

Remove any remaining bones with a very sharp knife. even commercial fillets may require this treatment.

To cook *anago*, braise it, skin side down, 7–8 minutes in a boiling mixture of equal quantities (by volume) of soy sauce, *sake*, *mirin* and *sugar*. For still more flavor, broil the fillets after they have cooled.

Broil *unagi* fillets skin side first on a skewer, in kebab-size chunks. Next, steam the broiled *unagi* for about 5 minutes, then drain. Baste with a sauce of *mirin* and sugar – about 1 part sugar to 3 parts *mirin*, then broil again, basting 2 or 3 times while broiling.

If you continue to cook *anago* in the liquid mentioned above, until the sauce begins to reduce, you will get a very thick, syrupy, strong-flavored dark-brown sauce called *tsu-me*. Continue to cook the stock, adding a little more soy sauce, sugar and mirin if it gets too dry. The resulting sauce, which is also thickened by the gelatin from the *anago*, is frequently used to dribble over different kinds of sushi.

1 Scrape the skin with a knife to remove the slime. The direction of movement in this picture is from left (as you look at it) to right.

2 Slice out the ribs.

3 Remove the backbone.

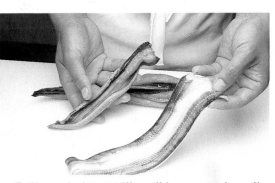

4 The cooked *unagi* fillet will be very much smaller than the uncooked version.

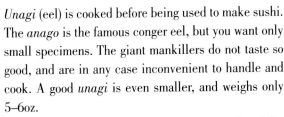

SHRIMP (Ebi)

Ebi (shrimp) is traditionally served cooked; only the very freshest 'sweet' shrimp is served raw.

The trick with cooked *ebi* is to keep them straight while they are cooking, and this is done with a very thin skewer inserted as shown. Stainless steel skewers are probably the most convenient, though bamboo skewers are more traditional. If you use bamboo skewers, wet them before use.

Wash the *ebi* thoroughly, then remove the vein with a toothpick inserted between the joints and the shell. Skewer the *ebi*, and drop them into boiling water. The *ebi* should sink at first, then rise to the surface when they are cooked. Scoop the *ebi* out, and drop them into ice water; this not only improves the color, but also makes it easier to remove the skewer. Twist the skewer as you remove it.

Peel the *ebi*, removing the legs and head but leaving the very tip of the tail intact.

Slice along the bottom of the *ebi* and 'butterfly' it, turning it inside out. Cover and refrigerate until used – and use quickly, because it is not easy to tell when cooked *ebi* have gone off.

Various kinds of shrimp are prepared for sushi. They have to be big enough to make it worthwhile, but small enough not to be unwieldy – no one makes crayfish sushi. Sometimes, you may find the ugly-looking but delicious mantis shrimp, which can be served raw or cooked. Raw shrimp are peeled and tailed in the same way as cooked ones, albeit with slightly more difficulty. You can use frozen shrimp this way, but they will need to be expensive, individually frozen shrimp, others will be too watery and flavorless.

1 Anti-clockwise from bottom left: raw *ebi* tail with bamboo skewer for cooking; cooked *ebi* with skewer; cooked *ebi* after removal of the skewer.

2 Peel the *ebi*. Traditionally, a small part of the tail tip is left on; cut at an angle like this.

3 Slice into the belly of the *ebi* without cutting all the way through to the back.

4 Turn the *ebi* inside out to create a 'butterfly' shrimp.

SMOKED SALMON

Smoked salmon is not exactly a traditional Japanese ingredient – indeed, it is commonly known in Japan by its English name – but, like so many other non-traditional ingredients, it works very well.

Use the fine, translucent type of slow-smoked salmon that is common in England (Scotch or Canadian smoked salmon), rather than the coarse chunks which are sometimes prepared in the United States. Slice finely, and use as sushi on Rainbow Rolls, as a garnish with roe or *uni* (sea urchin) or in any other way you think fit.

At the Yamato, a popular way to serve smoked salmon is in a Kosher Roll, with cream cheese and, according to taste, either *wakegi* (scallion) or cucumber.

At home, you can prepare Kosher Roll using economical smoked salmon pieces or pâte rather than sides or large fillets of smoked salmon. It is also an excellent way to serve sushi to people who do not like, cannot eat, or are afraid of raw fish.

1 Using the basic technique for an inside-out roll, begin with cucumber or scallion or both.

2 Next, add strips of smoked salmon. Be fairly generous or the delicate taste will be overwhelmed by the other ingredients.

3 Cut cream cheese into strips about ¼ sq in and put them alongside the smoked salmon strips, then roll.

4 Cut the roll in half and put the 2 pieces side by side, then cut twice more to get 6 pieces.

T E M A K I

A popular *temaki* at the Yamato is Salmon Skin Roll, made from a piece of salmon with the skin attached. It is broiled from the skin side.

The broiled salmon is cut into strips.

A half sheet of nori is spread with a little rice, then the salmon is added with vegetables as shown.

Because the rice is not tight-packed – a typical roll contains little more than a piece of *nigiri-zushi* – *temaki* are less filling than other kinds of sushi, and are ideal for people who are watching their weight. They may even be rolled in things other than *nori*: lettuce, especially Romaine lettuce, makes a light refreshing roll.

Like a number of other things in this book, *temaki* are a relatively recent innovation in sushi. They are hand-rolled *maki* made without the aid of a *makisu* (rolling mat). Nevertheless, they have rapidly gained popularity. In some Japanese sushi bars, customers can order a *temaki* meal which consists of a box of rice, a box of *nori* (seaweed paper) and an assortment of sushi ingredients, including fish, *kampyō* (dried gourd) and pickles. The customers then make the rolls to their own taste.

You can do the same thing at home. *Temaki* lend themselves admirably to a sushi buffet, where your guests can help themselves to whatever they like. Any of the ingredients described in this book are suitable, but you might care to offer tuna, a bowl of hot-pepper marinade, shrimp, *kampyō*, cucumber and, of course, *gari* (pickled ginger) and *wasabi* (Japanese horseradish).

Some people experiment with all kinds of other ingredients, such as cooked chicken, rare or raw beef, ham, cream cheese, *daikon* sprouts (white radish) and so forth. *Temaki* also offer a good way to experiment with ingredients you may not have tried before, such as *fuki* (boiled, salted coltsfoot, available in jars).

You can also use soft and semi-liquid ingredients such as roe or *uni* (sea urchin). In this case, it is easier to make the *temaki* slightly cone-shaped, with the rice at the bottom and the filling above it. Half-sheets of *nori* are easiest for this, though for buffets, quarter-sheets are arguably more manoeuverable and convivial, because people cluster around and make more of them!

The roll is somewhat conical, so the ingredients peep out of the wide end of the cone.